LEND ME YOUR FIRE

LEND ME YOUR FIRE

Poems of Love and Longing by Dead Society Poet

JR HATAWAY

JR Hataway

Contents

As always, for Rae
The girl with sunrise in her eyes

Swing Low

A gathering of whispers
these visions in time
let me linger a bit longer
amongst fondly held imprints
of midnight bliss
where you
draped in moonlight
and a daisy chain crown
swing low like the willows
and teach the roses
how to bloom

Wonderland

So many nights
spent staring at the sky
weaving poetry between
here and the moon
tasting dreams
along the edges of you
angel in hypnotic sway
lost in our own wonderland
spilling ink with
every star that falls
it took your love
to tell me who I am
I've always gotten it wrong

Photo: Holcy

Follow Me Down

Diamond dreams
razor reflections
whiskey heart
such a fool for you
sweet poison epiphany
no intention of slowing down
forgotten halos
now just broken rings
so follow me down
leap into the lost cause
of our own dark comedy
and love me
like it's our last day on earth

On The Run

Lascivious smile
turning the page
but no tome of spells
did she require
savage magic
in those emerald eyes
was more than enough
to set me ablaze
sending my demons
on the run

Drift In Silence

Making my way
along the sun-drenched shore
murmuring waves
echo the hum of my mind
reflecting sea glass
sparkles in obscure light
shards and scales
slice at my feet
hopes fade
like blood into the sand
stepping lightly
through so many razor-sharp regrets
biding my time
let me drift in the silence
when the tide rolls back in

Photo: Joshua Sortino

Wreck Me

Weary of insomniac storms
my mind all over the place
so often failing to recognize
baggage that I carry
murmurs amongst the undertow
taunting rhythm of the rain
relentless guilty pleasures
cloaked in your love
wreck me in your beautiful chaos
misery sure loves company

Flirtatious Addiction

Anticipation in blindfolded darkness
bound by this flirtatious addiction that is you
How do I say no?
a virtuoso performance
of exquisite agony
contorted to the twist
driven by the tempo
I just pray you don't
play me cruel
we HAVE to finish
what we started

Envy

The sky is working its magic again
a kaleidoscope of stars
in the dusty Milky Way
falling stars rain in heaven
as the cold mad moon
sends her midnight kiss
whiskey tears of envy flow
jealous of the nightflyers
so much closer than I'll ever be

Free

That luminary light fell to earth
like I fell for you
the night our curiosity
gave way to urgency
my heart set free from its cage
captured in your velvet embrace
a dance no longer confined to dreams

Another Second Chance

I dance between
strikes of lightning
upon thundering sands
soaked bones
at the chime of midnight
only fools waste
another second chance
swing to me
on yesterday's chains
hide away
listen to the world
no longer to simply exist
we'll echo in the heavens
like colliding summer storms

Photo: Melody P

Never Enough

Heart on fire in summer rain
damn this spell I'm under
what I lost tonight
echoes in the depths of letters I write
I prefer my pain dusted in moonlight
chasing dragonfly threads
as I dance on ivory thorns
forever is a long time and never enough
but maybe you'll still dream of me too

Moonlight Delusions

Midnight poetry
and the accompanying ache
holding on in the dark
slow sips of each memory
leaving me to dance
in moonlight delusions
savoring the tears
that still taste of you

No Words

No words to be said
in moments like these
between the power of that smile
and the weakness in my knees

Introduce Me to God

Salty eyes and singing tongue
serenade on the scarlet wind
a taste of sunshine
in the dancing shade
hold this swollen sin under your gaze
a drunken sailor to your thirsty shore
unfurl the world in this elegant enigma
and introduce me to God

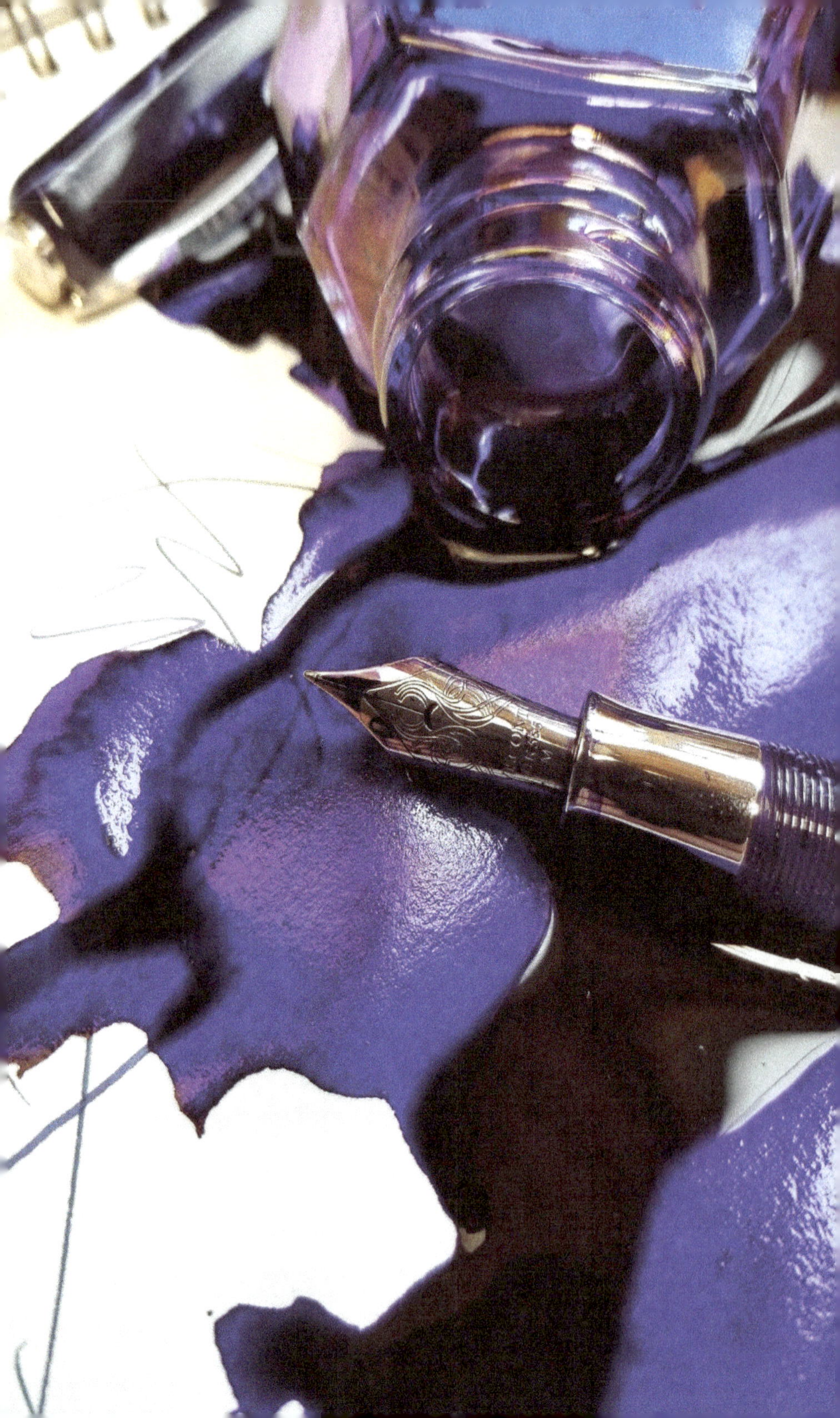

Crash and Burn

Crash and burn
regretful bones
fragile wings
a naked human at your feet
Will you bless the dark of this tired soul?
closed eyes to this mystical verse
lyrics of me in a chorus of you
let the rain find us dancing
poetry in forlorn flames
truth bleeds from a pen dipped in poison

Photo: David Pennington

Jealous of Your Mirror

I'm jealous of your mirror
and its front row seat
to each revolution
of my world

Dancing Out of Fear

My pen conspires with the moon
and old wounds healed too soon
spilling poetry of faded dreams
broken reflections of elegant failures
the mirror cannot hide
gasping for air
I battle a bursting sea
with its riptide of mockers
dancing out of fear
to a song that still breaks my heart

Up In Smoke

Let the words I've bled
go up in smoke
we'll find poetry
in the ashes
after I dance
in the fire with you

Love's Singing Ghost

I cling to the dark
grief of age borne out of time
my soul restless in silence of entirety
the flaming butterfly
dances a rainbow at my window
his whispers cloaked
as shadows in the wind
I rage at the sky with another patch of words
this misery of my own design
drowning the pain in the mists of moonlight
love's singing ghost in a cruel mirage
I must forgive the stars
a karma unscripted
and let wishes pile at my feet

Salvaging Words

Staring at the sky
praying I'll be given
another chance to dream
heart embroiled in fight or flight
tracing the moon's signature in fertile soil
let my soul sway with the wild naked flowers
painful punctuation to love
left out to pasture
salvaging words in a fusion
of unwritten ghosts
and roses yet to bloom

Strands of Love

Though I dance alone
so light on my feet
upon the quicksand of time
it's never for long
I draw back the curtain
at the edge of night
drunk on twilight
between shadows and stars
heart on fire in vermilion strands of love
your song tearing the sky apart
in a comet's trail

Catching the Wind

Draped in blue
I unravel in the mystic
shedding my skin
for the ghost of my dreams
she ministers the moon
in congregation with stars
a thousand colors of fire in her eyes
her golden cadence
in rhythm with my fleeing breath
catching the wind
like painted birds
on the wildest wings

Photo: Amir Hossein

Handmade Moon

Hold me hostage in the savage love
and sting of your pen
set your teeth into my bones
your bayonet tongue
savors the gunpowder of my blood
ink falls like rain on this sweet hell
spilling fickle musings on dusty pages
rip out the pain
and stuff my wounds
with black market flowers
decorate these scars in sinful poetry
as devotion starves under a handmade moon

Silver Sanctuary

In our silver sanctuary under the stars
we found a new Eden
sweet sips of breath
in a poet's hideaway
your voice pouring gold into thin air
a song I crave in a perpetual loop
telling me your dreams
in lyrics only you and the moon
know how to sing

Bleed the Melody Dry

Drowning in the wrong rain
another idiom of a foolish tongue
the bourbon cork crumbles
in the withering sun
rock my soul like a storm
with your song of fire
as we bleed the melody dry
swinging so wildly
into the comfort of night

This Side of the Truth

Memories flicker like candlelight
in the corners of my dead house
running empty halls
letters home never mailed
now poison my poetry
bitter disposition in sweet wine hell
pointless to weep in mourning
how love is often short
but forgetting is always long
though love bites dry
this side of the truth
I dangle hope on a heartstring
and dance away the pain

Melody Of Wonder

My heart falls in rhythm
to her melody of wonder
as those singing eyes
revel in the stars

Warm Our Youth

Days go by in a slow kerosene burn
with haggard heart and tired soul
I search for truth in the rain
until I'm drinking the wind to dry my bones
penning memories of your feathered voice
praying the stars relay my invitation
back down to my empty door
where you find me
in shy shadows of love's ghost
and we once again warm our youth
in a midnight blaze

Heavy Is My Prayer

Robed in darkness
heavy is my prayer of deluded truths
just let me dance in love's ardent flame
catching blue notes of the moon
in the palm of my hand
I live and die between each verse
grazing lips in the naked meadow
under circling stars
hold me down to disappear here
until we fall awake into broad daylig

Mocking Tomorrow

Time slips away
its poetic farewell in profound whispers
we pay the price of youth
in brittle bones and curling photographs
adorning the future
in gunpowder and doubt
so possess me in the now
layer my morning in birdsong
and dance for me under a guilty sky
I spike my coffee with a taste of you
mocking tomorrow
by planting roses in the ashes
of everything that burned

Diamond Night

I mold these words
into a shapeless fable
my world a mosaic of hues
drinking sunshine
from a brown bottle sky
folding myself into bygone dreams
let the universe conspire
to steal my faith in magic
as long as you dance in the diamond night
the candle of my soul will burn
like wildfire on the wind

Unspeakable Shore

Where shall I go?
As if I have a choice
forever you've bound me
in the prettiest chains
an imposter hero far from home
let me serenade you
to the sounds of the sea
on that unspeakable shore
where hell's wind silences the birds
and the stonecutter
carves love letters by moonlight

Fall Apart

Play me your sweetest melody
and watch me fall apart

Rhythm of Your Name

Familiar ground burns my feet
war waged between heart and mind
bleeding words and broken pieces
in dusty volumes of paper and ink
succumbing to the wear and tear
of hourglass sand
tyrants and fools plot to steal our joy
poisoning the marrow
tying our tongues of dissent
divinely we stumble through a fruitless garden
where starving birds wait to pick us clean
so bless me with your song
in the painted light of dawn
I'll dance between the empty graves
to the rhythm of your name
for at least another day

Safe Harbor

Songs of sorrow steal my breath
upon a swirling sea
bless me in the dark
delirious spirits burn my throat
the moon hides behind the rain
washing me clean of ash and blood
the buoy's noble bell rings in my bones
as I write my poetry by thunderstorm
seeking safe harbor only to drown in you

Worth the Risk

The sky stopped moving and
the stars spilled their secrets
ghosts of the sea
thumped the clouds and
mourned the swinging moon
I set fire to the old me and
danced upon simmering sands
let my apologies wither on the vine
burning alive at the stake of love
was worth the risk

Rapture

Sweet surrender to that thing you do
my salacious partner in crime
twisted tendencies in nefarious fusion
golden shots of midnight whiskey
slurring my words
twisting my thoughts
howling bare for my muse
white thighs of fury
a ladder to fire
my welcomed rapture into
cherry blossom heaven

Tragically Yours

Ambivalence tips the scales
with wringing hands
razor regrets I can't let go
you break me open to touch my heart
your music illuminates
slowly creeping in through the empty door
congealing time
as we make our wine of windfall fruit
this love, born of a dream
and tragically yours

Thief of Joy

Horn bellows like the devil's sigh
to all the lights of the dancing shore
breathless sails stall against the current
time's angst, that thief of joy
and missing links of the anchor chain
nibble of pride, grieved in stolen flame
my love nowhere in sight

Love's Drunken Shore

She channels the moon
amplifying the night
my verses ribboned around her torso
thrumming in balletic rhythm
in our whispering ears
as tongues melt
to the taste of misty moonshine
we burn the truth
and muddy the waters
dancing in braided lust
on love's drunken shore

Midnight Instrumental

Let the moon bear witness
bisecting our shadows
bathed in the fury of your salty kiss
forgetting my own name
in a midnight instrumental
cling to me as the sea hugs the earth
we rise and fall like the tides
filling the pages of a story
they'd surely ban in book form

Stranger to Hope

Internal screams
of gloomy-eyed fury
bleeding heart
indigenous to the hurt
treason is justified
for such a stranger to hope
so strum your chords
on the frayed heartstrings
leashing my demons
we'll sing to the youngest stars
until our tongues are numb
don't worry...
I'll embellish the story tomorrow

Borrowing Your Magic

We brawl in smoldering grass
threatened by our own joy
scarlet angels cry tears in shame
murmuring lullabies of eternity
through a haloed thrum
hopelessly I fall
to your incendiary carnal kiss
borrowing your magic
I burn like the sun's tears
kicking the devil's ashes
to the wind

Savoring the Ache

We meet on the thirsty shore
ragged sea of a dream
drunk under a vineyard moon
bleeding whispers drip
in vague intimate sonnets
frayed threads of temptation
curl my toes and cushion my fall
flanked by stars
we drink from the night's cup
savoring the ache
to the very last drop

Just Out of Reach

Out of my dreams
I stumble into the day
a recurring moment in a
symmetrical loop in time
I see her dancing
intoxicating whiskey saunter
through cinnamon mists of morning
my flirtatious addiction
just out of reach
like the moon teasing dawn
around the bend

The Mirror's Shadow

Bind me in your spell
save this old heart from itself
you weave verses
from a single kiss of magic
reluctant in who I have become
a saver that still needs saving
I won't ask again
just hold me down
in this gravity of souls
I'll take cover in the mirror's shadow
and maybe the moonbeams
will no longer burn my eyes

Magic Carpet

Teased by salvation
always seems just out of reach
so roll out your magic carpet
clench me in yearning
let the wind blow down our bones
as we tear the sky apart
the devil's dancing
among the stars tonight

Tear the Sky Down

There's beauty in the chaos
of this poetic love
blistered tongues
on whiskey wisdom
setting heaven on fire
every time I tear the sky down
and dance in thunder for you

Leaning On Time

Bless me with your kiss
let me get lost in you
I cling to each minute
leaning on time
slowing it down
whiskey hearts
beat in rhythm
with each breath
of an opal moon
hold me tight
anchor me to the real
and squeeze every drop
from the night
before the sun's
ranting fire of dawn

Lightning in a Bottle

Losing myself in the hypnotic sway
unable to deny
what brought me here
bound in your midnight charm
fingers laced beneath a curious moon
lightning caught in a bottle
you wear the night like a gown
shedding at dawn
taking sips of sweet morning dew
straight from rainbows in the haze
the sun warming my back
as we dance to songbird blues

Fall Like the Angels

I mend the words
of this hand-me-down heart
on lovelorn paper
jaded for so long
chasing yesterday's empty promise
tired of falling apart
so veil this hurt in your golden smile
swing down from the sky
and fall like the angels right into me
revel in the taste
of what the night brings
where stars no longer hide
and the moon spills light in our bones

Photo: Gantas Vaiciulenas

Burning Question

I live inside melodies
where only you know the words
glassy dreams of rapture
borrowing diamonds from the sky
blow the dust off
these boxed up pages
cut them open
twist your golden knife
trace the barbed wire scars on my soul
answer the burning question
and you'll see the song remains the same

All I Have

Greeted by bleak faces
in spiraling mist of morning
the shadowed ones that
guard the wall of hollow truths
drenched in amethyst haze of
whiskey earth tears
memories burn like fire
with each nail in the coffin
I won't apologize
for putting love on a pedestal
it's all I have

Arrogant Flame

Meet me in the meadow
where the road dwindles
sipping the moon
my words tied in knots
dancing to whispers of the night
falling asleep on a bed of flowers
no longer captive to
fear of the next heartbreak
let your love fall like the rain
douse this arrogant flame
drown me in you

Photo: Christian Bass

Fever

Let me hide from the world
and encapsulate my words
in dusty bronze poetry
another song unsung
my name on your lips
beckons me away
from the edge
so lace me up
in your ribbons
of midnight grace
moonlit tears always dry
under the blooming sky of dawn
setting fire to my ragged soul
a fever I hope will never break
I just love the way you burn me down

Fury

Hovering over the
peaks and valleys of
her lustful landscape
a torturous game
of touch and go
her quivering sighs
incendiary ignition
carmine nails dig in
drawing the fury down

Draped in the Night

Worshiping the words
of every song you sing
draped in the night
moonlight in our blood
stealing my breath
dancing in what might be
until dawn finds us
among the dogwoods
in all their charm
goodbye my sunrise companion
let me down easy
killing my history
left scars on my soul

Burn This Silence

Shine your light into the darkness of me
I turn to you to burn this silence
my words fail me
in silken reverie of your song
I'm falling too hard to sing along

Ocean of Ache

It doesn't matter what I do
during those nameless hours
in the velvet arms of night
dancing in my words
by the light of the moon
poems and songs
fall as dulcet prayers
across a quiet ocean of ache
barely rippling the surface

Bottled Up

Hide me away in the safety of your fire
shelter me from the cold mad world
bottled up in fear of what they want me to be
dragging chains of doubt
thumbing for rides on the road home
through trial and error
and watered-down whiskey
I've learned I'm not equipped to do this alone

Kiss of Heaven

My poet's heart
takes refuge in the stars
their dusted trails an alibi
bent to the cosmic sway
at the edge of night
I disappear inside myself
to wander in circles
a lost soul without a grave
looking to the sky
hungry for the moon's touch
hiding from the pain
in a kiss of heaven

Forbidden Fire

Silence broken
the hollow moan
of a faraway train
pounding earth and steel
in midnight revelation
our hearts drum
with the sound of the world
and every little thing it has to say
undeniable
like the temptation of sinful love
we jumped right into forbidden fire
falling...
wild-eyed...
right into destiny

Midnight Angel

So nimble she dances
along iridescent trails
taking her place
among the midnight angels
dancing in moonbeams
spotlighting her charm
a gypsy soul ablaze
in the dead of night
spellbinding wit
behind those green eyes
consumed in the fire of endless yearning
I howl with the wolves in gratitude

Her Psychedelic Soul

Enchanting stardust
of the Milky Way
splashed across the night
pulled such poetry
from her psychedelic soul
the moon and I
could only stare in wonder

Remember That Night

I will forever
remember that night
praying the moon
could bail me out
for words I couldn't say
our dance of lust and laughter
in our dreamer's hideaway
the night I carved
our initials in that tree
when this tarnished soul
learned to sing out of its chains
and words bled for you
came easier than breathing

Photo: Jeff Nissen

Dancing on the Winds

Alone in the forest
lost in her sky
touched by the moon's carousel of shadows
elasticated reflection of slanting light
memory of a dream
her song still echoes
dancing on the winds of firefly storms
grinning like a devil
my chaotic heart
stitched in emerald threads of wild delight

Drowning In You

Give me the strength
to harness these feelings
half-written pages of silent screams
beg for resolution
daydream illusions
bloom from scribbles
a balm to my weary soul
watering my roots
drowning in you
I find your love in every dawn
as long as the roses
sing your name
I'll belong to you

Beautiful Chaos

Wait for me
the night calls us home
as the angels cry watercolor tears
of a pastel sky
we linger in the frequencies
under their wings
untold stories shatter and bloom
in beautiful chaos of moonshine magic
oh to live and die in your midnight kiss
falling into you
my broken-hearted savior
pleasantly crashing
like there's no tomorrow

My Friend Loneliness

I've become friendly with loneliness
lingering here to let my scars breathe
with every heartbeat
loose from yesterday's jaded hope
writing the dark
woven static illusions
become black stone ballads
gone are the nights
spent resurrecting the past
thunderous denigration
that once fell like the rain
now lands like feathers
on a fading breeze
I raise a glass to ghosts
thankfully back in their graves

Angel of the Fog

There's a half-hidden path
known only to me
ferns and deadfall
make it difficult to see
I take a long stroll
when the moon is right
down to the river
in dark of night
She's always there
on the other side
dancing in the light
no reason to hide
I want to call out
but my voice is a loss
it's far too wide
to ever swim across
Accepting my plight
I take a seat on a log
watching her drift
my angel of the fog
Then in a flash she's gone
I'm back in my bed

dawn's light not helping
the pounding in my head
Rubbing my eyes
as reality crashes in
Damn..
it's that same dream again

Tricks on the Mind

I swear I saw you
in the mist tonight
Ruffled owls chorused
in orphic melodies
echoing your name
Cimmerian undulates
of ghostly haze
dawn arrived
burning away
undressing my surroundings
nothing here but this ache for you
it's funny how a heart
so crazy in love
sure can play tricks
on the mind

In the Wind

I see you in every field of wild daisies
gracefully dancing in the wind

Photo: Andreas Kretschmer

Sunday Morning

I woke this morning
sun streaming in the window
her bare back shimmering
a honey gold
I don't need to attend
your sermon on heaven and angels
I can describe both
in exquisite detail

Mere Mortal

Sipping her coffee
wearing my shirt
her form silhouetted
by the morning light
content in her reverie
I shouldn't disturb
but this urge
is just too much
for a mere mortal like me

Taking Flight

Metal wings
silver and white
carrying you away
taking flight
carving misty trails
into opaque sky
I pray the sun above
dries the tears of goodbye

Delicate Fire

Strike of the match
whiffs of sulfur
holding it close to guard the flame
such a delicate fire
can spark an inferno
for your heart I'll do the same

Heart On Parole

Moonless evening gives way to midnight
combing the pages of smeared ink
such a tenuous hold on a slither of a dream
hint of a smile behind an angel's green eyes
the devil chews the bars of his cage
if these walls could talk
they'd echo every tear
a heart on parole has cried

Ode to Etta

Analog hearts in a digital world
shelves of vintage vinyl
irreplaceable relics
the needle's hiss they found irresistible
rhythmic to the sway of genuine nostalgia
in a slow twirl around the room
the voice of an angel shook the ceiling
as two souls born out of time
dreamed of a bygone era
*Inspired by Etta James

Calling My Bluff

Soft winds play the front porch chimes
a timeless melody in bittersweet harmony
to your song etched in my heart
willows hang down
their dulcet sway
like your dress as I twirled you around
calling my bluff
forcing me to admit
I lied every time
I said I was happy alone

Rescue Me

Left to claw my way out
another mess I've made
languidly crawling
in chains of trepidation
not a moment's rest
soaked to the bone
in the slow rain of doubt
a burning heart and cool fancy words
my rescue flare fired into the night
fly with me to where the rainbows weep
and your song ignites the sky
where our own constellations
are woven in our dreams
that celestial love
is all that will save me now

The Devil Wins Again

Her lascivious smile
promises mischief
my eyes feast upon
the irresistible
risking everything
over nothing short of bliss
no match for this
collision of wills
the angel looks away
as it's abundantly clear
the devil on my other shoulder
has won this time

Folds of a Rose

Entranced by the lamp's dancing flame
circular shapes cast through glass refraction
adjacent walls hold shadows of love shared
giving in to dreams
flowing waves in our meadow
dancing flowers of your soul
welcoming petals
craving eternal embrace
poetry in the folds of a rose

Photo: Vadim Sadovski

Acknowledgements

There are so many in the writing community that I should thank. Your encouragement and friendship mean the world to me and continues to drive me everyday.

Also to everyone that took the time and spent your money to pick up A Walk After Midnight,
I cannot thank you enough!

Most importantly to my love, Rae, thank you for putting up with me. You are the embodiment of patience and love. I love you.

I thank you all from the bottom of my heart,
DSP

About the Poet

JR Hataway (Dead Society Poet) spends most of his time as a towboat captain on the inland rivers of the United States. He found a love for poetry and prose after discovering the works of Jim Harrison, Charles Bukowski, and Dylan Thomas along with many others. When not on the water you will find him somewhere along the backroads of Alabama with his dog, Petey.

Cindy Holloway